PEACE

BY

PIECE

Maria (Miller) Rockhill

WESTBOW
PRESS
A DIVISION OF THOMAS NELSON
& ZONDERVAN

WestBow Press books may be ordered through booksellers or by contacting:

WestBow Press
A Division of Thomas Nelson & Zondervan
1663 Liberty Drive
Bloomington, IN 47403
www.westbowpress.com
1 (866) 928-1240

ISBN: 978-1-4908-7637-5 (sc)
ISBN: 978-1-4908-7638-2 (e)

Library of Congress Control Number: 2015905675

Print information available on the last page.

WestBow Press rev. date: 4/13/2015

This book is lovingly dedicated
to my parents
Paul and Martha Miller
Their willingness to serve God
wherever it took them
wrote this story.

F o r e w o r d

While not all the events in this story are recounted in the chronological order in which they occurred, they are factual. Others will no doubt remember particular details differently, but I have written this as accurately as I remember it.

Maria Rockhill

Acknowledgements

To my husband, Steve. Your unwavering loyalty, love and support have meant more to me than you will ever know.

To my children-Steven, Andrew, Katrina, Emily and Nicholas. You are five of life's most precious gifts. Each of your imaginations could write ten books.

To my siblings – Hilda, Eldo, Margaret, Katrina and Eric. We lived this adventure together. You are the pieces of my heart's puzzle that will always firmly interlock. I love you.

To Doris Miller, one of life's first friends at Poplar Hill. Your keen memory and invaluable editorial assistance, so graciously and freely given, have helped move this book from dream to reality. Thank you so much.

Contents

Chapter 1

A NEW PUZZLE

"We're moving to Kansas?" Why is my voice barely a whisper when inside my head it's all screaming?

"Why do we have to move?" Daddy had already tried to explain it to me. Mama tried again. How it happened when we visited Kansas and he was riding on one of my uncle's tractors, out in one of those blowing, dusty fields. That's where Daddy was when God told him He wanted us to move. I just know he wasn't listening right and I didn't want to hear any more so I ran stumbling into my room. I knocked some of my puzzle pieces on the floor and slammed the door shut. Throwing myself on the bed, I squeezed my eyes shut. Hard. Harder. It didn't help. The tears came, warm and salty. I licked the salt off my lips and rubbed my eyes.

Staring into the blackness, I watched the rain. It was coming down hard, smacking against my window, and running down the glass. I shivered and pulled my pink bedspread around my shoulders. My thoughts rushed and tumbled faster than when we go sledding down the hill beside our house. I pressed my face into my pillow until they slowed down. When I looked up again, my pillowcase was soaked. My eyes wandered over to the calendar on my wall. There was an "x" on September 9, 1974. Did I just write that this morning? There was that salty taste again.

Someone knocked on my door. I knew it was Mama. Her knock always asks, "Please?"

"Come in," I said, my voice all squeaky. She opened the door slowly. Her eyes were red and crumply at the edges, like they looked when she had to fly to Red Lake for my brother to be born and we stayed behind.

She was wearing the blue sweater that matches her eyes. She sat on the bed, hugged me warm and didn't say anything. We talked like that for a while because you don't always need words to say something. Then she sat up straight, gently squeezed my arms, looked right at me and said,

"Maria, moving is like a puzzle. When you live in one place, you know what the picture looks like and where all the pieces fit. When you move, you have to put that puzzle away and get out a new one. Sometimes it takes a long time to make all the pieces fit, the pieces get all jumbled or they just get lost. The picture on the new box always looks different than the old one."

Mama bent down and started picking up the puzzle pieces I'd knocked down. She put them back on the square, wooden table where they were before. It's the table that fits all the Memory cards just right, if you line them up in straight rows. Then she said,

"You might want to walk away and give up when you can't make the pieces fit, but you have to keep trying."

I thought about that. Mama knows about moving. I have five brothers and sisters and she lived in a different house each time one of us was born. Daddy came in and sat on the bed. Then Mama said,

"Just think, the most important pieces of the puzzle won't change. Our whole family will move together. We can help each other make the pieces fit." I nodded, but my mind was still all jumbled up. Daddy and Mama kissed me soft on the head and left, closing the door gently behind them. I lay there for a long time, trying to get my thinking to go straight, but I couldn't. Finally, I fell asleep.

Chapter 2

DORIS HAS A SECRET

When I woke up the next morning I jumped right out of bed. I had just remembered something--Doris. I had to tell her. We play together a lot because she never got any sisters, just brothers. When I move, she'll have to find someone else to play with. I got dressed as fast as I could and asked Mama to braid my hair. I tried to sit still until she was done.

"You're a wiggle worm," she laughed as I ran out the door. I could see Doris coming from her house and running toward me. We met right in the middle of the campus beside the red, green and yellow merry-go-round that's between her blue house and my white one. Her eyes were all sparkly and her shoulders were hunched up. We looked at each other and waited. She started first.

"Guess what? I have to tell you something. We're moving." I couldn't even believe it. Then, she told me something I couldn't believe even more, "To Kansas."

4

"Me too!" I told her. I felt like I was going to explode. I had to ask, but I couldn't even swallow.

"Where?" Kansas is big. It could be anywhere.

"Partridge? No, maybe Hutchinson, I think." That's exactly where we're moving. She was going to have to make a new puzzle, too. We giggled.

"Can you believe it?" I asked her and she shook her head. We ran down the hill to the fence because today the airplanes are going to bring all the other students that didn't get here yet. We can't start school until everybody's here. I know who's coming for third grade because that's mine. Harry, Levi and Fabian already came from Osnaburgh yesterday and Murphy from Lac Seul. So, Adam still has to come from Cat Lake and Donna from Slate Falls.

The rest of the students will come and fill up all the other grades from one to nine. Planes will fly in from Deer Lake, Pikangikum, Fort Severn, Round Lake, Ear Falls, Sachigo Lake, Wunnimun, Mile 50, and some other places I can't remember.

Doris and I stood at the fence that ends right before the path leading down to the dock where the airplanes fly in. You have to wait until people come up from the dock. You can't go down. Mama makes sure we follow that rule because she can't swim.

"Do you hear it?" Doris asked. I shook my head no, but I wasn't really listening because I was staring at the Berens River. It's the shade of blue that goes all the way to the bottom, reaches all the way up into the sky and across to the reservation where the forest fire burned down a lot of the trees this summer.

The burned part reminded me of what Kansas looked like when we visited there. There were hardly any trees. It was hot and the wind blew and blew the dust around and it sounded like a song going up and down. Just like the forest fire when the smoke made those swirling black clouds that covered the blue part of the sky. Then the helicopter landed with all those chopping, moaning sounds and blew the sawdust everywhere when he landed near the sawmill. That fire just kept on burning and we had to pack our suitcases in case we had to fly to Red Lake. I'm really going to miss that blue piece in Kansas.

"Here it comes!" Doris's voice jerked me back from remembering. We watched the plane land, the pontoons spraying the water up, white and high. The pilot stopped the engine and the airplane started floating toward the dock. The propellers stopped spinning. I breathed a sigh because you have to stay away from propellers. Donnerbenner was a dog at Poplar Hill and part of his ear got whacked off by the propeller. After that, one of his ears looked even along the bottom instead of scoopy like the other one. Daddy got too close one time too and the propeller knocked his hat off. If it had been his head, he wouldn't be here anymore. I'm glad he was wearing a hat that day. Really glad.

The students kept flying in all day long. Daddy's the principal, so he was at school getting ready. Mama was in the school office, talking to the pilots on the two-way radio, to make sure everyone landed safely. They both came home smiling and Daddy said:

"Guess who brought in a couple of the flights today? Mr. Mitchell. Now there's a good pilot with a level head on his shoulders." Mr. Mitchell used to be a student at Poplar Hill. When he grew up, he became a pilot and now he's flying students in on airplanes like he used to ride in when he was a student here.

"Everyone likes to fly with him. He's a cheerful sort." Mama agreed. "Well, everyone's here now, safe and sound." Mama likes everyone all tucked in. So, now we can start school tomorrow.

Time For School

Poplar Hill is almost an island, but not quite. It's that word that sounds like pencil. Daddy told me how it started. A medicine man named Mr. Strang, a leader of the Midewiwin tribe, brought his family to live across the lake from where our school is now. Before those 1900 numbers.

"Mr. Strang's family were the first people on this peninsula." Daddy explained it to me. Oh yeah. Peninsula. Daddy always remembers the right word the first time.

"Later on, people like Mr. Schnupp helped to get this school started across the lake from Mr. Strang's village."

Mr. Schnupp went to college with Daddy and he was principal here first. Then, he needed to go be a missionary teacher somewhere else, so he asked Daddy to come and take his place. That's how we moved here. There was no tractor that time. Just Mr. Schnupp.

Daddy made his special breakfast this morning because it's the first day of school. I could hear that omelet sizzling in the big, black skillet. He whistled and Mama hummed to match. I was wearing my new bright green dress with the pink and yellow stripes. I took a big bite of those eggs and tasted all the flavors Daddy cooked in there. I didn't even know what they were, but I was ready for anything after that.

I walked down the hill to school and my stomach felt all twisty like it always does on the first day of school. Good twisty. I marched past the school sign that says, "Poplar Hill Development School, Established in 1962," and right through the front door.

The first person I saw was Miss Good. She does all the typing stuff at school and she was standing there smiling like the sun just came up. Warm, gentle and barely peeking over the trees.

"All ready for school?" She talked to me like I mattered.

"I can't wait!" I grinned, smoothed down my braids and my skirt and skipped to the end of the hall right into the junior classroom with all the other second, third and fourth graders. Doris was there too because she's in second grade this year. My teacher, Mr. Butikofer, turned when I walked in. His eyebrows went up and he kind of licked his lips in that funny little way he has. He never got married yet and his hair always looks rumpled even though he combs it.

"Well, good morning, Maria." His smile is the kind that makes you know he's really awake. "I'm going to have you sit by Fabian this year." He showed me the desk where I was going to sit. We sit by grades and Donna is the only other girl in my grade so I almost had to sit by a boy no matter what. Why do boys always smell dusty? You know, like they just ran all the way? Then, the school bell rang, so we all sat down and waited. Mr. Butikofer stood at the front of the classroom, cleared his throat and I knew exactly what he was going to say because he was my teacher last year:

"Good morning, boys and girls." That's how he always starts so I knew what I was supposed to say next:

"Good morning, Mr. Butikofer." You say the "fer" part like it really matters. He took out the dark blue Bible storybook and before he began to read, he pressed the pages down really flat. It helped him get started.

He read about the Israelites walking through the desert to get to Canaan. Boy, those Israelites sure complained a lot. They told their leader, Moses, that he was too bossy and that they were hot, hungry and thirsty. Well, what else would you be in a desert? Today, we read about the time a whole bunch of quail flew right into their camp and they just whacked them dead, so they would have meat to eat. That whacking part would have been fun.

As I listened, I looked around and saw the same papoose tikanoggin, the beaded mukluks, the snowshoes and the crossbow that were on the walls last year. Mr. Butikofer got them from different reservations and hung them up just straight. I wonder what will be on the classroom walls and who my teachers will be in Kansas. Those pieces will look different, for sure.

Our first subject was math and right away I knew. It was still like that Red River cereal we eat for breakfast sometimes. It takes a long time and it's good for you, but you sure are glad when it's done.

I was really just waiting for science, though. We all were, because Mr. Butikofer is the best science teacher in the whole school.

"We're each going to make a rock collection this year." he told us right off when we finally got to start that class. "Ontario has so many different kinds. You need to learn as much about them as you can." Then, he took us outside to show us different kinds of rocks and how we could tell what they were.

Like if they had a funny streak, or you could almost see through them and the ones that looked like someone tried to slice off a piece. When we came back inside, he went to the blackboard and spelled the names of the rocks he showed us--granite, mica, quartz and gneiss. That last one sounds like "nice," but it sure is spelled funny. I can't remember what kinds of rocks Kansas has.

Then, he showed us his special book on rocks. Some of them sure start out rough and ugly on the outside, but then they get polished up and shiny and you can't even tell it was the same rock. Most of those rocks aren't at Poplar Hill, but those pictures are so pretty. I want a book like that.

11

Chapter 4

GARDEN HARVEST

I ran right home when school was done because walking just takes too long. Our house is about halfway up the hill to the dorm. It's the one where daddy's cane hangs beside the door because his leg gets sore if he walks too much.

"Who's there?" Mama called out when I came in and slammed the door. I grinned:

"Nobody." Then mama called me her "shnickelfritz" because I'm really somebody, but I don't like to be called that German word. I think it sounds like a boy with a nickel in his nose.

"I'm really going to need everyone's help today," Mama came to the kitchen where I was getting a glass of milk. I stirred the milk powder into the water really fast so it looked like a little whirlpool in my cup. "Tonight is harvest at the big garden, so I'm going to need all my helpers."

All means me and my brothers and sisters--Hilda, Eldo, Margaret, Katrina and Eric. They're all older than me, except Eric. He's a baby, so he's just going to watch. When everyone else came home from school, Mama put us right to work:

"Hilda and Eldo, you grab shovels. Margaret and Katrina, you each take a five-gallon bucket and Maria, bring along those burlap bags. Daddy will carry your little brother." We all walked along the trail that leads back to the garden. It was a long walk so we sang along the way.

Music is always part of what we do and it makes me feel all warm and zingy. We sang "Home on the Range." I thought about Kansas and I wondered if there really are buffalo there, like the song said. I just remembered seeing lots and lots of cows that were black with white spots. Well, maybe it's the other way around. I don't remember.

Then we sang, "Deep in the Northwoods." Doris's dad, Mr. Jay, made up that song about Poplar Hill. Just the words, though. Somebody else wrote the music part.

When we got to the garden, I just stood and stared because I forgot how big it is. There are enough potatoes and carrots to feed everyone at school through the whole winter, so there's a lot of digging to do. Everyone at school helps with harvest and I started putting potatoes in the sack after Daddy dug them out of the ground. Eldo was helping some of the intermediate boys in another row but I think they were throwing more dirt than really digging vegetables. Hilda was with the senior girls. They were putting those vegetables in bags and buckets as fast as they could and rolling their eyes at those boys and calling them lazy. I couldn't see Margaret or Katrina, but I'm sure they were together, like usual.

Daddy stopped to talk to Mr. Howe. They were talking about bombardment games in the gym, because Mr. Howe teaches sports. The dirt was starting to get under my fingernails so much that I took a little break. I don't like when dirt feels like that sound you hear when someone takes their fingernails down the blackboard. It just makes me shiver.

I really wanted to see the Midewiwin graves at the edge of the big garden anyway. They sure don't look like my grandma's grave in Kansas. Hers is a gray, cement round hump sticking out of the ground that has her name on it, the day she was born, and the day she died.

I had to walk through some grass and really look around but finally, I found them. Midewiwin graves look like a little, flat house made out of wood that covers the ground where the person was buried. There's always a trail from the grave down to the lake. That way the dead person's spirit can go somewhere else. You never block the trail. EVER. Sometimes, there are toys or gum on the little house for the person who died. I saw some gum in a bright green package and I just wanted one piece. I took one little bite, hardly even big enough to taste, and I saw Hilda come marching over. I don't even know how she saw me.

"Maria, you put that gum back RIGHT NOW. You're not supposed to touch anything on those graves." I don't know why. The dead person sure couldn't chew it and we hardly ever get gum. Oh well. I put it back. Hilda kept right on talking even though I was all done listening.

"You should never disturb these graves, even if it's different from what we do, because it shows respect." Wow, I guess I'll leave that gum alone from now on. I went back to helping Daddy. He was still talking to Mr. Howe so he didn't even notice that I left. When everything was all dug up and put in bags or pails, we walked back home. No singing this time. Daddy carried Eric because he was asleep. Eldo told Hilda,

"I'm not lazy. We bagged just as many potatoes and carrots as you did." Hilda just stuck her nose up, made a little sniffing noise and kept walking. Margaret and Katrina were telling each other a secret. I think Hilda forgot to tell Mama and Daddy about the gum because they didn't say anything about it. Whew.

At bedtime, Daddy read a chapter from a Winnie the Pooh book about an expedition to the North Pole. Winnie the Pooh thought he discovered it, but he really didn't because he found it in the middle of a summer picnic and everybody knows the North Pole is freezing cold.

Kansas will be an adventure too, but I think the only poles there are telephone poles and they're not hard to find. Everywhere you drive, they're right beside the road. Daddy tucked me in, kissed me good night and whispered,

"It's going to be okay, Maria." I thought about Donna sleeping in the dorm and not having her mom or dad there to kiss her good night. The last thing I remembered before I fell asleep was that it was the first day of my last year of school at Poplar Hill.

Chapter 5

SO MANY BIRTHDAYS

Daddy's been a principal ever since I was born. That's not going to change when we move, but school sure will. See, it's not just about the tractor. We're moving so Hilda can finish high school and not have to leave our family like the students at Poplar Hill do. She's in grade nine this year and that's where Poplar Hill stops. Daddy's going to be the principal at Hilda's new high school. Daddy's always been my principal, so having a new principal will be a new puzzle piece to fit.

I think Doris is worried too because her dad won't have the same job when they move to Kansas Mr. Jay fixes a lot of things at Poplar Hill, but Doris doesn't know if he'll have the same job in Kansas, so she's kind of scared about that. We'll both go to the same new school, so we'll really have to stick together.

One thing that won't change about school is Columbus Day. Today Mr. Butikofer was talking about

Christopher Columbus. He showed us on the map where Columbus bumped into America by accident when he was really trying to sail to India. Mr. Butikofer showed us one of those old maps Columbus would have used. It was before they knew what the world was supposed to look like and the continents were all these funny shapes and sort of squished together.

The man who made that map had a really funny name-Ptolemy. Except you don't say the "p." I guess that's kind of the same thing as the ptarmigan, the bird that turns white to match the snow and brown to match the dirt. Then, Mr. Butikofer said:

"It's amazing he found anything at all." That's for sure. Then he asked us, "Does anyone know the names of Columbus' three ships?" Well, you bet I do, because one of those ships has my name in it. I raised my hand straight up and said that answer right out loud,

"Nina, Pinta and Santa Maria."

"Excellent!" Mr. Butikofer pronounced that word all sharp, so my answer felt just right.

I was still smiling when I ran home from school. I saw Eldo and told him about the ships. He's trying to turn into a teenager and he's always reading, especially Hardy Boys books and encyclopedias. Guess what he said?

"I don't think 'Santa Maria' is a good name for a ship because 'Santa' means 'saint' and you aren't one." He reads too much.

Well, I was sure done with him and I could smell something baking so I went to the kitchen. Then, I remembered. Today was the birthday party for Mama and Hilda because their birthdays are close together. Mama was born on Columbus Day, but not the same year as he discovered America or she would have died a long time ago. I guess her birthday is a pretty big number though, because she didn't want all the candles on her cake for how old she is.

"I have a secret to tell you," Mama said. "Judy is coming to visit as a special surprise for Hilda's birthday, so she's going to be here for a few days, while Mr. Schnupp is visiting some of the reserves." Really, when she says "reserves," she means reservations.

I smiled at Mama, but not inside, because I knew what it meant if Judy was coming. Judy is Mr. Schnupp's oldest girl and when she visits, Hilda acts all different. They sit on Hilda's bed, write in their private journals and read boring books where people smile funny at each other before they get married. They laugh and if I want to know what's funny they say,

"Oh, Maria, you wouldn't understand. You're only eight." They walk softly with their shoes and comb their hair for a long time, even when all the tangles are gone. Not me. I can't wait for Mama to get my hair combed so I can run and play.

Well, Judy came and I was right. After she left, the ice started to slush up and freeze.

THE NEW PIANO

You can't fly in or out of Poplar Hill until the ice is really frozen or you might fall through. Daddy and Mama always talk about how Katrina was born during the ice freezing up. It was a happy sad time for them.

They weren't living at Poplar Hill yet. They were living at Round Lake and Mama had to fly to Red lake for Katrina to get born because Round Lake is like Poplar Hill. It doesn't have a hospital. Daddy couldn't go along because he had to stay home and take care of Hilda, Eldo and Margaret. Mama couldn't fly back to Round Lake until the ice was frozen enough for an airplane to land so Daddy had to wait to meet Katrina until she was six weeks old.

One of the best things that ever happened after freeze up was when I was seven and we got a new piano. It was better than Christmas. They had to use a DC-3 airplane and the ice had to be at least three feet thick before they could fly it in. I saw that airplane land because I was watching and watching from the living room window. I knew I had to wait till they brought it up to our house, so I thought of something to do until it came.

Mr. Schnupp has a girl close to my age, Cathie, and she was visiting me when it came. She doesn't waste time combing her hair either. I remembered Mama laughing one time at someone who said something funny.

"That man is such a cut-up," is how she said it. I thought she liked it. I got Mama's scissors and started cutting up the green living room curtains. I was bubbling inside, all the way to the top. Cathie and I were just giggling.

When Mama came into the living room and saw the curtains, her face made all my bubbles go away so fast. Even faster than lickety-split. Her mouth kind of fell open and her eyes didn't blink at all. So, I found out that cutting up does NOT mean using a scissors on curtains.

Well, at least I haven't done anything bad to the piano and I play it and play it. I make up songs I can't really sing or play again. It's too hard to remember. So, I just play different notes the next time. The more I play, the faster the notes run from my head down into my fingers. I'll never be done playing.

We won't take the piano with us because you can only fly it out on thick winter ice and we're leaving next summer. I know you can make music fit anywhere you go, but I'm sure going to miss our piano. That will be a hard piece to put back into the box.

Chapter 7

A VERY MERRY CHRISTMAS

The closer it gets to Christmas, the better. Last night, we went to Doris's house to listen to "Amahl and the Night Visitors" and make different kinds of Christmas cookies like thumbprints, candy canes, molasses crinkles, snickerdoodles and sugar cookies. Mama and Mrs. Jay told us:

"Why don't you girls roll out the sugar cookies into different shapes and decorate the tops with frosting, sugar and candy?" Doris and I liked the cookie dough even better than the baked cookies, but we made sure Mama and Mrs. Jay weren't looking when we tasted some. For supper we had chili, crackers, dill pickles, bread and butter and lots of cookies. When we were all full, Mrs. Jay said:

"Time to gather around and listen." So we sat in the living room and Mrs. Jay handed out the papers with all the words for "Amahl". Then, Mr. Jay turned on the record player and we read all the words typed on those long pieces of paper that Mr.Jay had stapled together. The writing was purple.

It was one of those stories where they sang all the words and their voices always wiggled just right. There was this poor boy that had to walk with a crutch. Some rich men came to his house on their way to see baby Jesus. The best part was where those rich men told Amahl to have some licorice they brought with them. That's when Mr. Jay passed around a bowl of real licorice and said,

"Have some," Just like they did in the story. Well, except Mr. Jay didn't sing. I liked the red kind better than the black. The black made my nose turn up.

She's too polite to say it, but I think in school today Mama's ears didn't like what she was hearing, just like my nose didn't like that black licorice smell. We were working on our Christmas play and Mama's in charge of the music. One of the students wasn't singing the right notes, so Mama had him play the triangle instead. After that, I'm pretty sure her head wasn't tipping to the side as much. She does that when the notes are wrong.

In our play, I'm going to be a fairy that grants wishes. I have to grant a wish for Doris's brother, Curtis. He's supposed to make a wish to help other people instead of wanting presents and then I point at him with my wand and say,

"Your wish is granted." I saw my costume today and it's this white puffy robe with a funny belt. It doesn't

23

really look like the fairy clothes in our Grimm's fairy tale book but I don't really care because dressing up is way more fun than my regular, boring clothes.

After school today, Christmas carolers came to our house. It was some of the students and staff. Some adults make you stand outside their house and sing in the cold, but we always let people come inside. They sang my favorite one about the beautiful star of Bethlehem. After they finished we gave them cookies from the ones we made at Doris's house. This year they didn't taste as good because we left them in on the back porch too long and they were kind of frozen. Everyone said they were good and ate them anyway. That was really polite.

It's so hard to sleep when Christmas is almost here and tonight was the worst of all. It was Christmas Eve and I just couldn't. I kept looking at the clock. I checked and it was 2:05. I closed my eyes and waited and waited. Then, I opened them again. 2:08. It really was Christmas morning but I couldn't get up to open my presents until 5:00. Somebody knocked quietly on my door.

"Who is it?" I whispered, because I knew it couldn't be Mama or Daddy. They were sound asleep.

"Katrina and Margaret," they whispered back because they didn't want Mama and Daddy to wake up. They sleep in the basement and they came upstairs because they were wide awake too. They weren't really supposed to be upstairs, but they're not really up if they're in my bedroom.

They crawled into bed with me and we lay there, waiting and whispering about what we thought we might get until it was finally time to get up. Then, we ran right to the kitchen table because that's where Mama and Daddy always put our presents. I saw my plate first, filled with fruit, peanuts still in the shell and different kinds of candy. I ate the candy first. My present was beside my plate like always. I couldn't believe it. Mama and Daddy bought me a new doll. I couldn't stop looking at her and touching her shiny, gold hair. I know just what I'm going to name her-Sally Amanda.

Chapter 8

MR. SCHNUPP
COMES TO VISIT

1974 turned into 1975 and when one year changes into the next one, it's really winter. We couldn't even play outside yesterday because it was forty degrees below zero. Your face can freeze really fast on those days. Even when I just stuck my hand out the window for a little bit without my gloves on, I could feel them start to hurt and itch.

Today was a little bit warmer, so we played in the snow. It wasn't the right kind of snow to make a snowman. Too fluffy and blowing around, so we went sledding on the hill right between our house and the home economics house. I screamed and yelled every time I bounced over that big bump on the hill. The crazy carpets are the best for that and I felt just like I was flying.

Then, Katrina yelled that it was her turn and I needed to share, so we switched and I used the toboggan on the other part of the hill and that's not as fast, but it was still fun. I did it over and over again, even though I knew that tomorrow I'd have funny sore spots on my arms and legs.

Another thing that happens after the new year starts is that Mr. Schnupp always comes to visit. He's a pilot, too, and he and Daddy go and fly to all the reserves to visit the parents of the Poplar Hill students. Daddy takes a picture of each student using that camera that makes the picture shoot out of the camera right after you take it. He takes those pictures with him to show to the parents.

Mr. Schnupp flew in and stayed at our house last night so he and Daddy could fly out today. When we were eating supper, Daddy said something that Mr. Schnuup thought was funny and boy, did he laugh. When Mr. Schnupp laughs, it's different from anyone else. You can't hear it. He kind of throws his head back and makes this huffing sound like he can't breathe in enough air, even though he can. Then his face gets all red, he kind of squeaks and his smile is so big. It sure is funny.

The best part about Mr. Schnupp visiting is watching him eat because he eats a lot. Last night we watched him put butter on his bread. I didn't use a ruler to measure, but it looked like it was about three or four inches thick. Mama never lets us have that much. If we do, she says,

"There in the wood, a piggy wig stood". It's from a poem. Mama said it's polite to let guests eat more if they want it, so she didn't call Mr. Schnupp a piggy wig when he took too much butter.

This morning Daddy and Mr. Schnupp took off in Mr. Schnupp's airplane that he flew in from Dryden. It's a good thing they didn't take the Pilatus Porter from Red Lake. That's the missionary airplane we always fly in and it doesn't smell too good. It has "Christ is the Light" painted on the side with a black cross on a black hill and red behind the cross.

When you get in and sit on the seats, they don't really feel like they're fastened down hard. You feel like you could go sliding. They keep the bright orange gas cans behind the back seat, so you have to smell that when you're flying. The best thing to do is hold the white sick bag the pilot gives you. You can take medicine for your stomach before you fly, but that tastes worse than throwing up. Don't eat fried potatoes for breakfast before you fly. We tried it once, and it didn't work.

I know Daddy is sitting up in the front with Mr. Schnupp and Mr. Schnupp doesn't even have gas cans in the back, so Daddy won't need the sick bag. They talk about all kinds of things when they fly. I asked Daddy one time what they talk about and he said,

"All kinds of things to make little girls ask questions." So then, I really want to know, but he never tells me.

Really, if you want questions answered, the best person to ask is my sister, Margaret. She knows how to listen and ask questions that make you ask more questions. She would make a good doctor. Not the kind that tells you how tall you are or how much you weigh because they don't tell you the truth anyway. They always tell you you're growing so fast when it's not true. Growing up takes longer than waiting for Christmas or your birthday.

No, Margaret would be like Dr. Narramore. He's the one who helped Mama and Daddy with some questions they had about what they were thinking, but I think he made them come to California to ask their questions. Anyway, Margaret will probably figure out her new puzzle faster than the rest of us because at least she knows what the questions are.

Chapter 9

Too Much Homework

After Daddy came back from his trip, we had Pancake Day. I know you're supposed to eat breakfast in the morning, but on Pancake Day we have it in the afternoon too. Miss Lebold's always in charge of it because she's the home economics teacher. The senior student girls made different flavors of pancakes and it was kind of like eating in a restaurant because you waited and they told you where to sit. I'd like to do that, but I'm not old enough so I watched Hilda. She had to wear a special apron and a little yellow hat that said "Pancake House."

"What flavor pancakes would you like?" Hilda had to ask me. Just like that. She was really nice when she said it. Sometimes, I forget that she has to make a new puzzle too. I looked at the list to choose from-pineapple, regular, blueberry and banana.

"Blueberry," I said. I always pick blueberry.

"How many would you like?" They made her ask that, too.

"Two," I said because I knew Mama would start to say the poem if I said, "Three." When she brought them to our table, they were so soft and puffy, I could have eaten five. Mama didn't even tell me how much butter or syrup to put on, so I smeared it and dumped it on, but not as much as Mr. Schnupp.

Pancake Day makes you feel all warm and full on the inside, but the northern lights do that for the outside. They just light up the sky in the middle of winter.

"Would you look at that? Aurora borealis. Wow, they're bright tonight." Daddy said it right in my ear last night when he wrapped me up in my blankets and carried me outside to look at them. I shivered when I saw them, not from the cold. Those lights were such a bright yellowy green, swirling and almost dancing with the sky. The sky was so black behind the northern lights, you could almost feel it.

There weren't any northern lights tonight, though, and it felt so dark. Every night I have to go to the dorm for homework. Homework is fun most of the time because I can sit by Donna or Doris, instead of a boy. The subject I'm not so good at is sentences and sketches.

This is how you do it. On a piece of paper with lines, you divide it into three even parts, across, not up and down. You have three vocabulary words at the top of the page. You write a sentence and draw a picture to show what the sentence means, one word for each of the three parts on the page. You can colour the picture, too. The drawing part is harder, because my stick people don't have the same size arms and legs, but I like to colour with my favorite colours-red and orange.

Donna likes to draw pictures of Slate Falls, her house, and her cousins. Her pictures look real, like the ones she draws in the sand when she tells stories about living on the reserve. She makes it look so easy. It's like watching Katrina when she draws. She can draw anything just by looking at it.

Well, during homework I had to use the bathroom and that's not good because you have to use the outhouses. I went out the back door and down the long, board sidewalk all the way to the end. Every step I took made a loud crunching sound on the snow. I didn't hear an echo, but I could have. That outhouse is so cold, long and big, with all those doors right in a row. You can only use the one that has your name on a list by the door. I finished as fast as I could, because if I didn't, the boogey man could reach up and grab me. He's not real, but it sure feels like it. I ran back to the dorm as soon I was done. I was breathing so fast.

At the end of homework I had to run fast again to get home. I ran past all those trees and hoped no bears were hiding. Bears are real and big. Last summer, when we were swimming at the sand beach, we saw one. He was big, brown and running away from us on the logging trail, but we ran the other way anyway. He might have changed his mind and started to chase us.

When I saw that bear, my throat got so thick I could hardly breathe. Doris's brother, Curtis, went to get the staff men to come and chase him away. Katrina ran after them and tried to help too, but Mr. Butikofer said,

"You need to turn around and go back. This is no job for a young lady." Sometimes I dream about that bear chasing me. He almost catches me, but not quite. Then, I wake up. I'm glad there won't be bears and outhouses in Kansas. Maybe there won't even be any homework. Those pieces will go right into the box and not come out again. Not ever.

Chapter 10

SATURDAY FUN

Mama and Daddy will be leaving soon for a couple of weeks to take the seniors on their class trip, so that means March is almost done. They're going all the way to Ottawa at the other end of Ontario. Mama showed me a map of how far it is. It only looks like a few inches, but it's really a lot longer.

"It's farther to drive there than to drive to Kansas. See?" Then she showed me how big Ontario is on the map and when I used my finger to go from Poplar Hill to Ottawa and then from Poplar Hill to Kansas, Kansas wasn't quite as far. Wow. It always takes a long, long time to get to Kansas, so they're going to be driving in those vans a lot.

I wanted to stay at the dorm with Donna while Mama and Daddy are gone, but I'm going to stay with Mr. and Mrs. Ken instead. He's the senior teacher and he's going to be the principal after we leave.

Mama, Daddy and the seniors are going to sing in a lot of different churches on their trip. That means they have to practice in the assembly hall on Saturdays. Since Mama helps with the chorus, I get to stay with Miss Lebold at the Home Economics house while they practice. I wish we could stay long enough for her to be my teacher. When I got there today, she was all ready for me:

"Guess what I have for you? A sweet little treat.' When she smiled, it reached all the way to her eyes and they crinkled at the edges. She took me to this little room she has with a desk and she opened the drawer where she keeps these flat, shiny candies. Some were white and some were green.

"Why don't you pick out two?" I took one of each and sucked on the green one first. Peppermint. My whole mouth felt just fresh and I blew it through my teeth like a whistle. Mama came to get me before I was ready to leave, but I didn't mind as much today because we were having another birthday party.

My baby brother, Eric, turned two today. I'm glad he wasn't born a day later. People would have played jokes on him and said "April Fool" and not really believed him when he said it was his birthday

After he was born and Mama brought him back from Red Lake, she walked up from the dock and right into the school, so I could see him. He was wrapped in a yellow blanket and he didn't have any hair. His fingers and toes were so little and perfect.

35

He's bigger now, but he still doesn't have much hair. I have to help fold all his white diapers and there are so many. Miss Betty, one of the cooks at the dorm, made a Snoopy face cake for this birthday. Snoopy is from Daddy's favorite comic strip, "Peanuts."

You should have seen Eric's eyes get big when he saw that cake. When he smiled you could see that some of his teeth were still missing. Mama and Daddy let him stick his fingers right into the middle of the cake and he just started laughing and smearing the frosting all over his face. I'll bet Mr. Schnupp would have liked that. I guess Eric won't remember too much about Poplar Hill.

After Eric's birthday party, we went to the assembly hall to watch some skits.

Mr. Butikofer is a really good teacher, but I like him the best when he does those skits with the other single staff men for the Saturday night programmes in the assembly hall. He's not the only one who isn't married yet at Poplar Hill and he lives in a special house for all the staff men like that. It's all the way across the campus from the not- married ladies' house. I think that's probably on purpose. But you know what? Even though they built those houses that far apart, those single staff still get married.

If you don't believe me, just go into the staff lounge at the dorm where they wait for the meal times to start in the dining room. I'm pretty sure I saw Mr. Eberly smiling funny at Miss King when I went to check our mail. Maybe Miss Martin and Mr. Beachy too, but I'm not sure. Maybe they read those books that Hilda and Judy like. Usually if they keep smiling at each other like that for a while, they get married. So, that's that.

Well, anyway, tonight at the assembly hall, the single staff men did some skits. Theirs are always the funniest and they put on a skit where Mr. Butikofer was just hanging out of the ceiling all upside down. I never saw him or anybody else do that before. His rumply hair was all wild hanging over like that and I was laughing so hard. Everyone clapped and clapped for that skit.

They did one skit Doris and I didn't like. They made it look like someone was bleeding right out of their head. Really, they used ketchup, but it scared me anyway. I hope they don't do that skit again.

The other fun thing to do on Saturday nights is watching films. The Tijean ones are the best. Tijean is kind of like Paul Bunyan, except he's Canadian. One time a storm was coming and he harvested a whole field before it came. I'll bet the people in Kansas would like him because he could harvest all those wheat fields without even using one combine.

Paul Bunyan's good too, but he didn't really finish his job in America. He kind of stomped through the top part making the great lakes and the ones in Minnesota, but he forgot to go a little farther down and put a few more in Kansas.

ALL ON A SUNDAY

I like Sundays because that's when we go to church. Eric doesn't always like it as much as he likes the Saturday night skits. He usually wants church to be done before it's really over. Singing is always my favorite part of church. One of the teachers, Miss Zehr, led the songs today. She's a good song leader. We sing before Daddy starts his sermon.

I forgot to tell you that Daddy is a preacher, too. Sometimes we sing out of the songbook and sometimes we sing the words Miss Zehr wrote on that big, white tablet she has set up in the front. That tablet is almost as tall as I am, and it sits on an easel. Her writing is all even and straight. When she smiles, it's kind of a straight line. Not mean, just not open all the way. You can't see her teeth when she smiles.

She blows into one of the little square holes in her round pitch pipe that's black on the top and silver on the bottom. That way you start singing on the right note. Then she waves her hand so you won't sing too fast or too slow. The way she waves is sort of choppy and stiff and it makes me think of a soldier marching with his back really straight.

I sit next to Mama while Daddy preaches. She's soft and warm. There's a picture of a face inside the front cover of her Bible that I drew when she wasn't looking. You can't erase it. When you open her Bible, it smells clean and strong. Just like her. She lets me draw pictures on paper and play with her handkerchief.

I fold it into shapes, especially the one where you make a triangle and roll it from both ends to make two little rolls. I call them the twin babies. If I had a twin, I would want it to be a boy, not a girl. That way he could tell me the secrets the boys say when they play that they won't tell the girls.

Chapter 12

THE BIG RAPIDS

Outside, it's turning into spring because I can hear the ice crashing around and so now I know it's starting to melt. You can really hear other sounds more clearly during break up. Like when Harry and Levi kept slamming the front door of the dorm and I could hear it down in Daddy's office at school.

We can work on a new collection in science too, because the snow's melting and we can collect more things outside. Mr. Butikofer is helping us make a wood collection. He knows a lot about trees like ash, pine, birch, larch, fir and poplar. We're putting them in a flat, Carnation milk powder box. It's brown on the inside, but bright red on the top with white letters. Each piece of wood is like a little rectangle about as long as your palm is wide.

"And then," he said, "We're going to varnish the tops. Just as smooth as you please." The best kind of wood he showed us is one that doesn't even grow in Ontario. It's cherry with the swirls in it. I'm going to keep my collection forever. Until I grow up.

Mr. Butikofer is teaching us other things about wood, too. Since the staff men and senior and intermediate boy students build all the buildings at Poplar Hill and most of them are made of wood, he taught us about the log booms.

The staff men bring them down the Berens River every summer. They chop down trees, throw the logs in the water and push them in a big group until they stop at the sawmill, right behind the school. Then, they push them up on the bank, let them dry, and cut them into boards using that big, sharp, shiny blade that's even taller than me. I'm so scared of that blade Mama doesn't even have to tell me not to get too close to it.

One blade I'm not so scared of is an axe and it's another good thing about spring-camping. You use an axe for different things when you go camping like cutting down branches for a campfire and splitting wood.

I was so glad when the ice finally melted, because then we could go camping at the Big Rapids. We don't always go, but Daddy said that since it's our last chance, we're sure going this year. I helped Mama pack all the food stuff and then we went down to the dock to get one of the motor boats.

First, we all had to put on the bright orange life jackets because if you fell into that water, it would still be really, really cold. We clambored aboard and I was afraid that boat was going to tip right over. I like to sit backwards at the front of the boat and watch the water spraying away from the sides and the white foamy stuff that comes behind the motor.

I heard the Big Rapids before we got there because they were roaring loud. We came around the bend and all of a sudden, there they were. The water just kept coming down over the top and it was so white and too fast to swim in. I just watched and watched.

We pulled our boat up on the rocks, got out the fishing poles, and started fishing right away. I wanted to catch as many walleye and northern pike as I could, so I used my favorite red and white lure that's shaped like a big raindrop. You always have to eat bannock with fish too.

Bannock is easy to make and guess what? Mama said I could make it this time. Well, I knew I could do it, but she never let me do it by myself before. I took flour, baking powder, salt and water and mixed them with my hands, nice and sticky. Then, I took lard and put it in a black frying pan over the campfire, until it was clear instead of white and it snapped in the pan.

I put the bannock dough on the snapping lard, fast and careful so it didn't burn me and fried it crusty and brown on both sides. I took it off the fire and waited until it cooled down a little bit before I put butter and strawberry jam on it. It tasted okay, but not quite right. Then, I remembered. Maybe I forgot to put the salt in after all. Everyone ate it fast, anyway. Bannock always runs out before you're full of it.

After we ate, we sat around the campfire, drank hot tea with sugar and Carnation milk and were kind of quiet, like we were all thinking about moving. I must have fallen asleep because the next thing I remember was waking up in my sleeping bag, the sun shining bright in my eyes and Mama singing. It was one of those songs she sings when she wants us to get up:

It's morning time in the bushland.
It's morning time in the bushland.
It's morning time in the bushland.
Wake up, my sleepyhead.

When we got into the boat and headed back to Poplar Hill, I kept turning around to look at those rapids because I don't ever want to forget what that piece looks like, even if I have to put it back in the box.

Chapter 13

FIELD DAY AND GRADUATION

Mama sure didn't have to wake me up today because it's Field Day. It's one the last things we do at school before all the students fly home. There are all kinds of events you can enter like running, shot put, pole vault, high jump and long jump. My favorite part is watching the staff men make the running lanes with sawdust from the top at the dorm to the bottom at the school. When everything was ready, Mr. Butikofer used his megaphone to announce the events. Running races is the best, so when it was my turn, I lined up in my lane and waited for him to yell,

"On your marks, get set, go!" I ran as fast as I could but Donna beat me again this year, just like last year. I think she runs even faster than the Kansas wind.

When Field Day was over, everyone had at least one ribbon. Hilda got one for running long jump. Eldo got one in shot put. Margaret and Katrina both got first place in the 50 yard dash. So, we all won something.

Then, it was time to get cleaned up for graduation. I couldn't find my dress shoes, so I went downstairs to look. Hilda was the only one down there and she was getting ready for graduation. I kind of didn't know what to say.

"May I come in?" She looked at me and smiled. She had on her white blouse and black skirt, like all the other senior girls are going to be wearing for graduation. She was pretty quiet and I think she must be remembering that we're moving soon.

"Do I look all right?" She turned around so I could see her from the front.

"Really nice," I'm surprised, but I meant it this time. Maybe we'll be friends in Kansas. It could happen.

"I think everyone else left. We'd better hurry," Hilda told me and her eyes almost looked wet. Then, we walked down the hill to go to the assembly hall for the last time.

Hilda and all the other seniors walked up to the front of the auditorium and sat down. Then, they got up and sang and Daddy talked, but I wasn't really listening because it all sounded far away and not quite real. At the end of the programme, Daddy had all the seniors line up and then he said each name and they came up and got their diplomas.

Each diploma was all rolled up and tied with a purple ribbon. It was kind of funny when Daddy shook a person's hand and gave them the diploma with the other hand because a couple of people got their hands mixed up It was nice to be able to laugh a little bit.

After that, the seniors all marched downstairs and lined up outside, I went down the line and shook their hands and said,

"Congratulations!" I couldn't quite say anything when I come to Hilda because my throat got all choked up, so I just hugged her a little bit instead. We went home and I was so tired I just went right to sleep and didn't even dream about any bears.

Chapter 14

UP, UP AND AWAY

Mama didn't wake me up today. The quiet did. It was so loud. For the last two days all the students were flying back to the reserves. I'll probably never see Donna again, but I'm glad she can sleep in her own bed. When I went outside and looked at the dorm, all those windows seemed like big eyes staring back at me and not seeing anything. Just black. Poplar Hill feels so empty.

It's our turn now. All our stuff is packed and our house is echoing because all the rooms are empty. Mr. and Mrs. Ken will be moving into our house soon. There won't be a cane by the front door anymore. Mr. Ken's leg doesn't hurt when he walks.

I walk through each room in our house and whisper "goodbye," especially to my bedroom. When I come outside, Doris is standing there.

"Do you want to play children of Israel one more time?" she asks.

"Yes!" I say because we like to act out the story that Mr. Butikofer read to us about when they ate the quail., Well, except we added a couple of things to the story that aren't in the Bible. We pretend like we ate too many quail and we throw up over our back fence. It's really fun to make all those throwing up noises.

Then, we pretend that we're the Israelite parents and our children don't listen to us. They run all over the desert and we have to chase them back into the camp. Doris and I played and played. We were laughing so hard, I almost forgot it was time to leave until Daddy called me,

"Time to head for the dock, Maria." I tell Doris I'll see her soon, because I will. I run down to the dock and my whole family's there. Mama's wearing her blue sweater. The dock is full of our boxes and suitcases. I hear the Pilatus coming and it almost sounds like a Kansas tractor.

Lots of things are staying here and lots of things are going with us. I step into the Pilatus for the last time, click my seatbelt and make sure I have Sally Amanda. I look up and I can't believe who the pilot is. It's Mr. Mitchell.

"Ready for adventure?" He grins. I grin back. NOW I'm ready to take off. Away from Poplar Hill and the maple leaf flag waving good-bye in the breeze. Toward Kansas and a flag with stars and stripes, blowing in the wind. There's a whole new puzzle waiting for me. For Doris, too. I just have to remember what Mama said.

If I keep trying, someday all the pieces will fit. Just right.

CPSIA information can be obtained
at www.ICGtesting.com
Printed in the USA
FFOW03n1923290415
13060FF

9 781490 876375